From the Heart of a Dreamer

From the Heart of a Dreamer

A collection of writings

By

Frank L. Nolan

Composed in San Francisco – Las Vegas – and the Caribbean Island of Aruba

Photo and layout by Kalix Muangchoo

From the Heart of a Dreamer

Note From the Author.

Hopefully among these works there is something for everyone. Most of what has been shared in these writings comes from the wonderful experience of the many who have touched my life.

Over the years, up until today, so many terrific people have been the source of inspiration.

Thank you all so much not only for the inspiration but for your help.

TABLE OF CONTENT

MOMENTS

"precious and

unbelievable moments"

-MOMENTS-

Moments are our only true reality.

What is transpiring now is all of life.

Life that comes at us one moment at a time.

Embrace and cherish them, those precious and unbelievable moments.

The sound of waves pounding on an Aruban beach.

The plunge into the ocean's water at Eagle beach.

The warm rain on your face in the middle of a tropical storm.

The first taste of a finely prepared cappuccino.

The flavor of a very sweet grape.

The aroma of that meal prepared especially for you.

The embrace of a great friend

An unexpected greeting from a passerby

The smile that says, you know I care.

Even that last breath, passing from this world to the next.

Let it not be just a moment of acceptance, but of joy.

Joy, for the mystery that awaits us all.

ENCHANTED GARDEN

"A warm gentle respite"

-AN ENCHANTED GARDEN-

Tender tears of joy,

the heart cries out in expectation.

Overwhelming in the moment of splendor,

The touch of an angel, felt in the deepest part of the soul.

Embrace me in sweet silence.

Be taken in by all that has come before.

Allow its presence to dwell in you.

No stranger here,

Only those who have not yet partaken in the wonder.

The visit may be brief,

A warm gentle respite,

With majestic view and fragrance from afar

Til next time may this place of enchantment hold memories

Sweet and poignant.

Never to be forgotten

LAUGHTER

"Laugh alone, laugh together"

-LAUGHTER-

So very powerful and healing

A wonderful gift

Laugh alone.

Laugh together.

Laugh at your defects.

Laugh equally loud at your strengths.

Laugh at victory.

Laugh also at defeat.

Laugh when you are sad.

Laugh a bit louder when you are happy.

Laugh at the enemy.

Laugh at your allies, but maybe just a little more joyously.

Just laugh until you cry.

Remember, it just life.

TOGETHER
"Travel with an open heart"

-TOGETHER-

Let each encounter be an opportunity.

As one slips by, there may not be another.

Be unafraid of what may come to pass.

Recognize it may be your last chance to give.

Give openly and freely.

Touch as many as possible; differences are removed when we travel with an open heart.

Remember, the least among us is joyously worthy of your presence.

So be there.

SERVICE

"Doing one simple thing for someone else"

-SERVICE-

Need we be reminded about the great joy of being in service.

Forgetting about one's own problems and finding something that you can do for someone else.

It does not have to be something monumental.

Service, like very fine wine, can be excellent in very small doses.

Just a simple "Hello"

"Can I get you a nice cup of coffee?"

"Would you like to take a short walk?"

"I just called to see how you are doing."

"Do you need anything at the store?"

"If you need a little break; I can help."

(Doing one simple thing for someone else)

Sounds pretty easy, maybe we should try it.

You may be serving yourself as well as another.

It may be your pain that is eased.

Someone once said, "Service is nothing more than putting love into action."

Sounds like something worth trying.

MR. EFRAN

"You will always come first"

-MR. EFRAN-

"He is a beautiful friend.

He will never let you down.

Always will he be at your side.

You will always come first."

Miss Ana's words after her first meeting with Efran.

Ana is my soul mate and one of those with scary intuition.

(Always aware before anyone else)

Yes, he was my dear friend.

Efran left us some years ago.

Having an unwritten bond between two men is special.

Just knowing Mr. Efran, special and unique

Saying so little, but giving and doing so much.

He always did walk a step or two behind.

As his friend, it was more about me and less about himself.

It has been awhile, but Mr. Efran, you are still frequently in my thoughts and always will be.

(In a very warm and wonderful way)

PASSAGE OF TIME
"Be kind"

-PASSAGE OF TIME-

I am getting tired.

Time is passing much more quickly than yesterday and I am getting tired.

It seems so little has been done.

And I am getting a bit more tired.

Just keep putting one foot in front of the other.

But, I am getting so very tired.

What else is there to do?

(Be Kind)

Until the last tic of the clock

FORGIVENESS

"It does not have to be hurried,

only profound willingness is neccessary"

-FORGIVENESS-

All hope and salvation lie in the power of forgiveness.

Without true forgiveness there can be no healing.

All acts of the betrayer must be met with forgiveness.

It does not have to be hurried; only profound willingness is necessary.

There is no need to forget, only to realize our shared humanity.

In the spirit of this shared humanity we come nearer to an understanding of our own imperfections.

In this spirit our betrayer becomes our teacher, the awful pain of resentment begins to leave.

We realize that all joy and happiness we desire for ourselves, we also desire for our betrayers.

We have started on a path to "Peace"

An inner peace which comes with true forgiveness.

LITTLE PEOPLE

"Fully in the present"

-LITTLE PEOPLE-

The big yellow balloon is bouncing from one small hand to another.

All eyes are on the unpredictable flight of the globe.

There is really nothing else, just a big yellow balloon.

For now that big yellow balloon is their world,

Not a thought about what came before or what is going to take place when it is gone.

Just the big yellow balloon

Will it get away from them?

Maybe take off into the big blue sky, gone forever, the big yellow balloon.

Only the big yellow balloon has meaning.

Living these few precious moments fully in the present.

Past and future are not allowed.

Not even considered.

Shall we take a lesson from these little ones?

Truly allowing ourselves that which is right in front of us.

"Lest we become like little children."

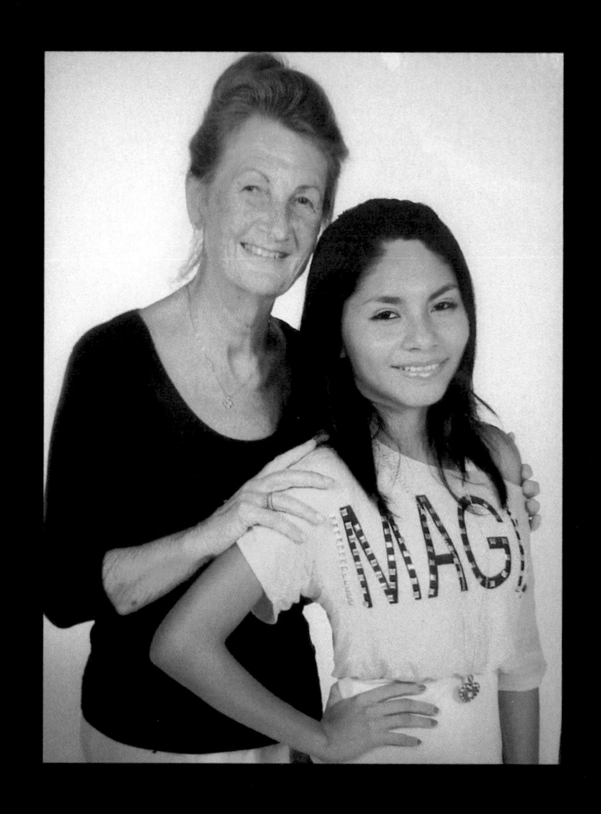

To Our Most Beloved Jos

A lasting union

-TO OUR MOST BELOVED JOS-

You are one of those who has been granted a very special gift.

A gift that over the years you have shared with so many.

Your generosity has given wings to this special gift.

A gift now truly inseparable from that wonderful person you are, a living part of your very essence.

The gift is a demonstration of an unselfish purpose, more meaningful than oneself.

You certainly have fulfilled this purpose, a testament to the many you have touched.

Yes, you have touched many, none so deeply and profoundly as the precious Angelica[1][2].

You bond is strong. Your union everlasting, and that gift to always be given away and shared, "The gift of love and service"

---

1 My God daughter – lives on the island of Aruba

2 Jos – Angelica's God mother.

RESPONSIBILITY

"leave the world a little better

than we found it"

-RESPONSIBILITY-

A hungry child in Somalia,

An earthquake in Haiti,

A neighbor who needs help with a sick child

All are part of our responsibility to mankind.

Are we able to see the universal need to exclude no-one from our dream of a better world?

Are we able to accept the pain and suffering of another so their journey may be a little happier?

Can we always try to see others as more worthy than ourselves? (An expression of both humility and solidarity)

Grant us the wisdom to see clearly our universal responsibility.

In doing so, hopefully, we will leave the world a little better than we found it.

WHO ARE

THE BEAUTIFUL PEOPLE

"We are all in this world together"

-WHO ARE THE BEAUTIFUL PEOPLE?-

Actually, just about anyone will do.

We are all in this world together.

So who says we should be selective.

It's all about time and circumstances.

Time changes everything.

Who you are.

Where you are.

What you think.

What you are doing.

So let us just enjoy.

Shall we dance?

Shall we sing?

Shall we play?

Always remember that you are one of the beautiful people too.

It's your world.

So make each and every day a celebration.

A UNION FOR LIFE'S JOURNEY

"Join hands and walk in the clear, brisk wind"

-A UNION FOR LIFE'S JOURNEY-

It is spring. Nature renews itself.

Enjoy the beauty and fragrance of it blossoming.

A new beginning has been given to you.

Summer bestows upon you its sunshine and warmth.

Frolic in the season's splendor.

Play like children in all that the season has to offer you.

It is autumn. The leaves are beginning to fall.

The chill in the air refreshes your spirit.

Join hands and walk in the clear, brisk wind.

Let it cleanse your souls.

Winter has so quickly come upon you.

It is the time of reflection.

How joyful and wonderful it has been.

Celebrate each day, your journey together; for all is reborn.

You will surely be together again.

ANA

"Always of some greater good"

-ANA-

She is so beautiful in so many special and different ways.

If you get to meet her, take the time, you'll be so glad that you did.

I have learned from so many, but I do believe more from this diminutive lady.

It is never just about her. It is always of some greater good.

She has great compassion for the less fortunate and all who suffer, always so mindful of the little things.

Her simple lifestyle and needs reveal a deep respect for all.

One thing for sure, the world is a much better place with Ana[3].

[3] Beautiful friend and wife over the last fifteen years.

A CALL TO LOVE

"Support and cherish each other's growth"

-A CALL TO LOVE-

When the call to love beckons, embrace its warmth and rapture.

Give freely and joyously into each other's hearts.

Let your heart open to the delicious splendor.

Sing and dance together, relishing love's sweetness.

Know also that to taste love profoundly is to experience pain of a tender heart.

For it in both joy and pain that the spirit is nurtured.

And if there is a divine purpose for your union it is to grow spiritually.

You were brought together not only to sing and dance, but to be part of the spiritual growth of each other.

Give to that growth, knowing that the journey must ultimately be taken alone.

Love intensely both side by side and from afar.

Support and cherish each other's growth.

Walking together in the spirit, but with separation.

For in union there is still need to follow one's spiritual path.

Support your beloved on this journey.

A journey of the spirit taken only with one's Creator.

DAD
"One of a kind"

Frank Louis Nolan Sr.

If there ever was a real John Wayne, it was he.

Just watch him enter a room and see everything change.

Mention his name and you could be sure people were going to listen.

Big and powerful, but also gentle and kind; it was a marvelous combination.

He was also a great defender of the weak and less fortunate.

Certainly, one of a kind

Never a bad or unkind word about anyone, there was no judgment in his world.

Everyone was fine just the way they were.

Gossip and any kind of slander were not permitted.

When there were unkind words spoken; he would simply say, "Oh Joe, well he is not such a bad guy"

Then there would be silence.

I wanted to be like him. He was the greatest.

Thank you dad

I always knew how much you cared and loved.

We both knew, but we never said it.

WILLIE

"Nobody did it like Willie"

Watching someone do something they love to do is enjoyable.

Watching the very best perform his or her craft, outstanding.

Watching the Say Hey Kid[4] do his thing in the dog days of summer, a once in a lifetime experience.

Just seeing him on that field you knew that he was where he was meant to be.

Like he was and always would be there.

Center field belonged to Willie. Other people might have played center, but it was Willie's home.

He played the game with such youthful exuberance. Having so much fun without trying that hard, he was just the best.

Nobody did it like Willie.

Going from first to third on a slow grounder to third.

The delayed steal on a casual throw back to the pitcher.

The routine single to right center becomes a double.

A head first dive into third, double now a triple.

The lost cap running down the long fly to left center, then making his patented basket-catch look easy.

No it wasn't the Polo Grounds, but you were still the greatest during your years in San Francisco

---

[4] Willie Mays - NY/SF Giants 1951-1952, 1954-1972, NY Mets 1972-1973

You were always the greatest.

The Say Hey Kid was born to play centerfield.

I am so glad I caught your incredible act.

LISTEN
Sometime that is all we need to do

-LISTEN-

The situation is really unbearable.

Everyone is extremely angry.

I believe that both my father and mother have forgotten why it is that they are so full of resentments.

Now all the anger and resentment are just like a bad habit.

Conversation about the news ended a few months ago. Now no one talks, just silence

It's not a peaceful silence. It is that silence that makes you want to run away.

Mom has her place in front of the TV with her cheap red wine. She drinks until she passes out.

Dad is in another room watching whatever ESPN has to offer.

My brother lives in the streets and checks in occasionally for food.

I just hope and pray it will get better, but my hope is fading. I need to get out.

"Three Months Later"

Mr. Nolan do you have a minute? You will not believe.

They have been in counseling for almost two months.

Things are changing. Last night mom and dad went out on a date.

When they came home, I could hear them laughing.

There is hope.

Thank you so much for all your advice.

I said nothing.

Allows others to speak their recovery.

Sometime that is all we need to do.

Listen with an open heart, without condemnation or judgment.

Amazing things may come to pass.

GOOD-BYE MY DEAREST

"beautiful and yet so fragile"

-GOOD-BYE MY DEAREST-

It was simply out of this world.

The fresh veggies were certainly great.

The perfectly seasoned tomato sauce was outstanding, and just the right amount of cheese.

All blended nicely together, just for dad.

Remembering that which was so very, very good.

Seeing that special child[5], so often hidden by fear

Now so beautiful and yet so fragile.

Warm, sweet, joyous tears

Yes, Father K, (Too gentle to live among the wolves)

This night, for an ever so brief moment, the fear is gone. There is only joy.

---

[5] Janene Michelle Nolan (7/28/1966 -9/25/1997)

A WONDERFUL WOMAN

"A Joyous presence"

-A WONDERFUL WOMAN-

A smile that lights up the entire island.

Laughter that makes you smile with your heart.

You feel like a small child on the eve of Christmas.

All the gifts have little meaning.

The real gift is the joyous presence of one very special lady.

Yes there is a sense of pain.

Wounds that have cut deeply into her very soul.

But a spirit still strong and powerful that will overcome.

An uncompromising faith deep and profound that says everything is in His Hands.

She knows so well that she is truly one of His special children.

Wonderful Gloria[6]...Enjoy the coffee.

---

[6] Gloria Rios – an outstanding student and source of strength and joy. Gloria was born in Columbia and now lives on the island of Aruba

THE LONG ROAD HOME

"Amazing journey"

-THE LONG ROAD HOME-

The leatherback turtle is hatched in Aruba.

He spends most of his time in the North Atlantic, sometimes over one hundred years.

Comes back to Aruba to die.

Point A to point B and back to point A

Amazing

The last year or two I believe I've been getting closer.

How does one know that he is getting closer?

What does it really mean to be getting closer?

Closer to what?

Some says home.

Are we really going home?

Home to What? To whatever comes next.

The journey certainly has been something, most of the time with so little understanding.

What am I doing?

Where am I going?

Never really feeling on course.

Then again, is there supposed to be a course. You start at point A and you end at point B.

I am not so sure.

Most of the time I started at the point A and I never make it to point B - wherever that is.

Even when I have some idea of where point B actually is I often find myself somewhere else.

Not so amazing.

John K. & Russ L.

PALS

Two of the best

-PALS-

Not many things greater than a real pal.

Whether good times or bad, always at your side

A helping hand extended when there was little hope.

You only get the truth.

Not the stark truth intended to hurt, but the truth tempered with compassion.

How sad that some people don't have one, a pal.

Even sadder, some people do not want one.

They chose to do this life thing alone.

I never would have made it, without my pals.

I was blessed to have a few.

Two were special and have been around for many years.

John K. and Russ L.

I write these words for you.

A Pal

Better than a sunset on a Caribbean Island.

Better than fresh bake bread.

Better than a last second shot in the big game.

Better than a beautiful, glorious, Latin wom- ....Well maybe not.

WE NOT I

"when you are weak, we will carry you"

-WE NOT I-

Together we can have success.

A concept which is so simple, yet, so incredibly profound.

When I am weak, you must be the source of strength.

When you are weak, I will carry you.

When we are both weak we must seek out another that we can help.

Then there will be three.

From there, we could become a group of four or more.

Always with the thought of helping another, our group can continue to grow.

Together we have the power to heal.

To take the emotionally and spiritually crippled and give them a chance to be whole.

Down the road we go finding others. Helping them help themselves, so they can help others.

The road becomes a highway.

The highway leads to a city, which becomes a state.

The state spreads to other states until the entire nation is covered, then the entire world.

Men and women around the globe, once very sick, now walking among the many with great dignity and purpose.

Where have I heard about this phenomenon[7]?

---

[7] The phenomenon is Alcoholics Anonymous. Founded in 1935

The concept sounds like something we already have.

Well, it was just a thought!

ATTICUS

"Dignity and Respect"

-ATTICUS-

I wish I could have had a cup of coffee with Atticus Finch.

There were people, when I was young that I wanted to be like. Then there were a few that went far beyond that hope. There was no way to achieve that type of goodness or greatness. Atticus was one of those.

Atticus and I met about fifty years ago in the form of Gregory Peck. I still have problems separating the two.

The epitome of strength, honor, and intelligence; but above all he was humble.

His many talents were just gifts. It seemed he took no responsibility for them.

Atticus just always did the right thing. How powerful is that?

In the face of the worst injustice, he stood firm in defense of an innocent man. And he did so with dignity and respect.

It was 1933, in the deep southern part of the United States. It was an older, all male jury. It all mattered little to Atticus. He just did the right thing.

"Summary of Closing Argument"

Tom Robinson is guilty only of feeling sorry for a poor, uneducated white woman… nothing more.

Tom Robinson belongs with his family. He has done nothing but come to the aid of someone who asked for his help. Reunite Tom Robinson with his family.

In the name of God do your duty.

Atticus knew the probable verdict, but that summary made it clear to everyone that Tom Robinson was only guilty of being a kind and gentle man.

It was Tom Robinson's compassion that made him break a long standing social norm. He felt sorry for a white woman.

Betrayed by this act of kindness, he was on trial for his life.

Atticus stood firm in the defense of Tom Robinson.

Racial heroism demonstrated so beautifully and powerfully

So much more to be said, however, I just say thank you both (Atticus and Gregory[8]) A simple expression of gratitude. Atticus, I am sure would be pleased.

---

[8] It was Harper Lee's great novel (*To Kill A Mocking Bird*) that gave us Atticus Finch – made into a motion picture in 1962.

IN LOVING MEMORY

OF MOM

Alice Elizabeth Nolan

(September 23, 1913 – May 7, 1990)